I0116240

Who is the
PREDATOR?

Warning Signs

Diane Roblin-Lee

Foreword by
Melodie Bissell

Predator-Proof Your Family Series – #2 *Who is the Predator?*
© 2017 Diane Roblin-Lee
First Edition 2010
Second Edition 2017
Third Edition 2025

ISBN 978-1-896213-01-9   E-book 978-1-896213-61-3

PUBLISHED IN CANADA
byDesign Media
www.bydesignmedia.ca

COVER DESIGN — Diane Roblin-Lee

Cataloguing data available from Library and Archives Canada

Disclaimer: The opinions expressed in this booklet are those of the author and do not constitute part of the curriculum of any program. The development, preparation and publication of this work has been undertaken with great care. However, the author, publisher, editors, employees and agents of Plan to Protect®, are not responsible for any errors contained herein or for consequences that may ensue from use of materials or information contained in this work. The information contained herein is intended to assist communities, institutions and individuals in establishing effective response to a controversial issue and is distributed with the understanding that it does not constitute legal or medical advice. References to quoted sources are only as current as the date of the publications and do not reflect subsequent changes in law. Where any sourced material may have been inadequately referenced, the author extends a apology. The research has been so extensive that it has been impossible to track every source. Organizations, communities and individuals are strongly encouraged to seek legal counsel as well as counsel from an insurance company when establishing any policy concerned with this topic.

Purpose

The eightfold purpose behind the
Predator-Proof Your Family Series:

- To help families and guardians recognize danger signs in
  people who have access to the children in their care

- To deter people who are fantasizing about molesting
  a child from acting on their fantasies

- To protect children from molestation through raising
  awareness on many levels

- To be aware of the new challenges of parenting in the
  21st century.

- To deepen the understanding of all levels of society affected
  by the molestation of a child

- To find healing for victims and families

- To encourage the kind of justice and community action that
  prevents potential or convicted predators from initial offending
  and re-offending.

- To demonstrate to all those who have been molested that
  we care deeply about what you have endured and, in honour
  of you, are doing all we can to protect other children from
  sharing your experience.

Predator-Proof Your Family Booklet Series

By Diane Roblin-Lee

Booklet #1 – *Why All the Fuss?* ISBN 978-1-896213-00-2
Prevalence, Effects and Trends of Child Sexual Abuse

Booklet #2 – *Who is the Predator?* ISBN 978-1-896213-01-9
Identification – Warning Signs

Booklet #3 – *Predator-Proofing Our Children* ISBN 978-1-896213-02-6
Recognizing the Grooming Process
Parent/Child Education – When the Molester Strikes at Home

Booklet #4 – *Predators in Pews and Pulpits* ISBN 978-1-896213-03-3
The God Factor - Forgiveness?
How Dare They Call Themselves Christians?

Booklet #5 – *The Porn Factor* ISBN 978-1-896213-04-0
Are You Raising a Predator?
The Old Bottom Line - The Buck

Booklet #6 – *It's All About the Brain* ISBN 978-1-896213-05-7
Does Child Molestation Affect Brain Development?
How to Use the Brain in Effective Treatment

Booklet #7 – *When the Worst That Can Happen Has Already Happened*
ISBN 978-1-896213-06-4 Healing for the Victim
Parenting an Abused Child – Coping as the Family of a Predator

Booklet #8 – *Smart Justice* ISBN 978-1-896213-07-1
Community Response to Predators Who Have Served Their Time
Church Response - School Response - Restorative Justice

Booklet #9 – *The Husband I Never Knew* ISBN 978-1-896213-08-8
The true story of Diane Roblin-Lee, ex-wife of a man who, after 38
years of marriage, confessed to being a child molester.

Available online in Paperback, Kindle and E-Pub
Also available through Plan to Protect®
117 Ringwood Dr., Unit #11, Stouffville, ON CAN L4A 8C1
www.plantoprotect.com 1-877-455-3555

Foreword

As a child, I was spared twice from a predator. One day I was walking the distance of 15 houses down the street from my friend Susan's home. A car followed me slowly. A man rolled down his window and invited me into his car. Frightened, I ran the remaining few meters to the sanctuary of my home. The second time, I was walking through a ravine with a friend when a man, who I had never seen before, exposed himself to us. Both of these incidences involved complete strangers – the proverbial "dirty old men lurking about!"

Now, as I travel internationally to speak and teach, I hear thousands of stories that begin something like this:

> "He was a friend of our teenage son...."

> "He was a gentleman who rented a room from us. We lived on the first level and he lived upstairs."

> "He was my husband for 40 years."

> "She was our babysitter."

> "He was my father – and he was also a pastor."

> "He was the children's pastor."

The stories are rarely about strangers. In most cases, the abuser was someone known well to the victim.

My heart never ceases to break.

We must use sound judgment and wisdom in raising our children, without living in constant fear and paranoia.

Mom and Dad – don't be too trusting. You have been given the privilege of providing the oversight and care for your children. As my friend Carol Wiebe (co-author and editor of *Plan to Protect* ®) said, "We secure our passwords, computer, bank accounts, vehicles, and phones. We deal with security and safety issues every day of our lives. Why wouldn't we want to do all that we can to secure our children and our youth?"

Melodie Bissell

President, Plan to Protect ®
www.plantoprotect.com

Who is the Predator?

Who can know the darkness of heart that dwells within anyone? Until outed through charges being laid against them, predators are usually impossible to spot. They lurk behind masks designed to look like everyman or everywoman.

My research for this series of booklets was not limited to libraries or news reports. Besides my own experience of being married (unknowingly) to a child molester for 25 of the 38 years of our marriage, I gained valuable insight from individuals who were willing to expose their hearts in interviews in hopes that their sharing would assist in the battle to protect children.

One of these contributors was my ex-husband. For the purposes of this work, I'll call him "Matt." He was a middle-aged professional man who lost his family, home, career, reputation, dignity, friends and sense of self-worth when charged and convicted of molesting two young girls and attempting to molest three others. While not an example of a sadistic pedophile, he is typical of a multitude of predators who started out dabbling in pornography and ended up destroying not only their own lives but many of the lives around them – and losing everything.

The devastation thrust upon our home was so complete that I determined not to allow it to happen without finding some purpose in all we went through. I began to wonder how any young mom could be expected to recognize danger for her children if I could live with a predator for 25 years and have no clue. While my lack of awareness surrounding the issues of abuse and predators resulted in my inability to protect my own family, I determined to share the insights so painfully gained in hopes that it might save some other children and families from abuse.

After struggling through mountains of research and writing the first draft of the manuscript for this series, I made copies and sent them to all the members of my family for their input. The response was varied because the betrayal had been intense and everyone was still suffering at varying levels of wounding and healing.

One of the positive responses came from one of my granddaughters who said, "This would be good, Grandma, except that all we're getting is your perspective. It would be more meaningful and helpful if we had Grandpa's perspective as well." I considered her words and was grateful for her wisdom.

After he was released from prison, I contacted my ex-husband and asked him how he would feel about an interview. He was broken and open to exposing his shame if it could, in any way, dissuade anyone else from targeting a child or acting on fantasies – or if it could in any way bring healing to his victims or give insight into the pandemic of child molestation.

He arrived one cold, fall morning at my apartment. After sharing a home for 38 years, it was awkward inviting him into my sanctuary. He didn't belong here, but I was grateful for his willingness to contribute to my work. I motioned him to a sofa that had once belonged to us both, and he sat down.

8

There wasn't a lot of small talk. I plugged in my equipment, hoping to glean insights that would help other moms to spot potential danger for their kids. The whole scenario was eerily other-worldly. How could this even be happening? How could 38 years together end with a cold, metal microphone between us? How does one take the leap from a marital relationship to a clinical interview? I had to ignore my inner turmoil and focus on the purpose of my work. I turned on the recorder and began.

D. Let's go back to the beginning. Where did this all start? What was the root?

M. Pornography was certainly a major contributing factor.

D. Was there anything else at the root of it?

M. Well, the absence of a healthy adult sexual relationship was not a good environment for me to be in.

D. How do you account for that? What was wrong with your relationship with me?

M. I think that on our honeymoon when I was more open about wanting to do the kind of stuff I saw in pornography, and I realized that you weren't into it, I disconnected and took the easy way out in more pornography and fantasizing and other relationships. We just grew apart. Instead of working on a healthy relationship, I replaced normal, healthy sex with more and more degrading pornography.

D. So you had no desire for normal sex ?

M. No.

D. Do you think that if I had willingly participated in all the weird things you wanted to do that you would never have gotten involved with the first young girl? Could I have prevented all this?

M. There's no way of knowing that. I never had any thoughts of sex with kids. All the time I was messing around with other women while I was traveling so much, it was all about adults. The thought of kids never crossed my mind. (*Note: During the course of his confession, "Matt" confessed to a seemingly endless number of affairs and sexual encounters with other women – even with my supposed 'best friend.'*)

D. *In terms of the root, do you feel that there was anything generational, or anything in you that led you to be attracted to children? Do you think you were born with that sexual predisposition?*

M. I don't think so. Psychologists have determined that I am not a real pedophile. Not all people who molest children are pedophiles. True pedophiles just go for kids. That is not my preference. I was always into adult sex but got involved with the two young girls because they were there and I was so selfish that I cared more about self-gratification than anything else at the time. I think that in both cases, with both girls, it was a matter of convenience. I was in a trusted position for a long time.

D. *When you were a child, did you have sexual experiences or were you molested by anyone?*

M. When I was about nine, I was molested by a counselor at a Scout camp. I called home and tried to get my parents to come and get me, but they didn't, and so I told the senior camp counselor. Then my parents came and got me. Other than that, there were about three instances of experimentation with other children who were older than I, but in talking with psychologists, they seem to think that those circumstances were just normal childhood curiosity.

D. *What did your parents say to you about it?*

M. We never talked about it. It was as though it never happened.

D. *Do you feel your abuse had any effect on your sexual development or your relationship with me?*

M. I don't know. It wasn't a good situation. I felt very ostracized at the camp because I was treated like the snitch who had caused this fellow who molested me to be sent home. Everybody was mad because this fellow had been very popular. They didn't know what he had done to me. I just wanted to go home, to get out of there. I was there for about a day before my parents came.

D. *Do you, yourself, feel that the incidents with other children were normal childhood occurrences – or do you feel that they had an effect on your development?*

M. It's not something that you can qualify. I don't know what I would have been like had those things never happened.

D. *Research speaks of the "grooming process" child molesters use to gain the trust of their victims and families. Did you intentionally groom your first victim with the intent of molesting her?*

M. While I had begun to fantasize about schoolgirls, I never intended to get myself in a situation of molesting a child. The first time it happened, I was leading a children's church group, and a young girl who was a foster child of a family in the church used to want to be around me all the time. She had been sexually active in a previous home and was very clingy with any male leader who would pay attention to her. She was mentally and emotionally weak and just wanted someone to love her. She wanted males to love her. One of the other leaders had to have a talk with her foster mother about how she was constantly making plays for the male leaders. I played on her needs. One day when I was at her home, she flipped her top up out of the blue and exposed her breasts to me. That's when I should have just told her to pull it down and left the situation, but I didn't.

D. *Did the foster parents not suspect anything?*

M. The girl's foster mother was very observant. I felt she was always on the outlook for the kids because she had had a previous situation where someone was suspected of molesting one of her grandkids, and so I never pushed anything, simply because that would have been a red flag to her. I could sense that she was always very protective.

D. *Did you ever feel that she had any distrust of you?*

M. No. Not at all. In fact, it was the opposite. I was very much in a position of trust with the kids.

D. *You must have begun to feel very isolated after all that began to happen. You became isolated from people who could have helped you. Can you talk about how that was?*

M. It just reinforced the behavior. It made me go deeper into unreality and interact more with the kids than with the adults. It was a real catch-22 situation.

D. *How did you see yourself in relation to other people?*

M. I always felt that in a funny sort of way I was superior to other people – that I was smart, that I was clever. I was getting away

12

with it. Did I like me? No. But deep down I always felt that I did a good job at a lot of things. I felt that there weren't a lot of people who could do certain things as well as I could do them. Believe it or not, I thought I was spiritually astute. That was a total deception, obviously. I was proud to the extent of being vain. Not a very nice person. I worked at trying to appear to be a nice person, but it was all a sham.

D. How long did that situation with that young girl continue?

M. I'm not exactly sure. She eventually went to another home in Toronto. Then there was a church party of some sort, and I volunteered to go to Toronto to pick her up, and that's when it ended.

D. Why did it end?

M. Because I took her to a secluded spot on the way and proceeded to molest her and she started to cry. That's when I stopped. I snapped out of it and took her home.

D. There were quite a few years between the first girl and our neighbor's daughter, Linda.[1] Why did you choose Linda?

M. I think Linda was the most vulnerable. She was always very clingy and wanted to be around me. She was at my house a lot with my grandkids. Linda was very bright, but she was emotionally needy because of her circumstances, and craved the attention. Other kids who were strong characters never entered my mind. Never even entered my mind.

D. How old was she when you began to touch her?

M. I think she was about ten.

---

1. An assumed name and relationship to protect the identity of the victim.

D. Was she frightened?

M. No, I don't think so. It began as a back rub and just progressed from there. In my mind, she was enjoying the attention. I was obviously rationalizing totally inappropriate behavior. It was totally about self-gratification.

D. So her discomfort wouldn't have stopped you.

M. No. The best thing Linda ever did was to tell because even though I stopped over a year before she told, I'm convinced that I would have started again at some point.

D. Your desires were progressive, then?

M. Yes. I never went beyond touching the girls with my hands, but towards the end, I was fantasizing about being touched and I know I was moving in that direction.

D. When you were touching them, were you physically aggressive? Did you force yourself on them?

M. I did with Linda. I wasn't violent, but I knew that she didn't want to do certain things and I did.

D. Would you have progressed as far as rape?

M. No, I wouldn't have forced her like that, but if she hadn't cried, I would have gone further and if she had given any inkling of wanting to participate – which I know was a ridiculous thought – I would have gone further. That's just how low my mind had sunk.

D. How old was she then?

M. She would have been twelve or thirteen. But in both cases, with both of the girls, when they cried and said stop, I stopped. I think

14

when they did that, they broke through the veil of being objects to me and became children and that's when I stopped.

D. When you were molesting a child, how did you feel about the child?

M. I didn't really have any... I think I felt that I was giving them pleasure, or that was what I told myself, which was of course not true. It was all about self-gratification. While I was touching them, I thought of them as objects, not as children. When you're doing that you don't think of them as victims. It's just as though they're nonexistent. They're not people. They're objects.

D. Did you ever have a real relationship with Linda? Was she ever a human being to you – or was she always just an object?

M. Oh no, I cared very deeply for her. It was only when I was trying to self-gratify myself that she was an object. But there were so many times when I felt so close to her. I was almost like a Dr. Jeckyll and Mr. Hyde. I was very deceptive. Extremely deceptive. There are perpetrators who basically target a kid on the street and use violence but that wasn't my thing. It wasn't anything I ever did or would have done. There was always something deep inside of me that said that wasn't ever going to happen.

D. What were your thoughts after you had molested a young girl?

M. Regret. Deep, deep regret. I felt very unworthy. Like a real heel. A real schmuck.

D. So after Linda cried, it never happened again?

M. That's right. It never happened again. And I think it was over a year before she reported me. If I hadn't gotten caught, I know I would have tried again. The victim needs to tell.

D. If she had been questioned, do you think Linda would have told about it earlier?

M. I think that communication from adults to the child is extremely important. Because I have a feeling that if anybody had sat down with Linda and asked her if everything was okay in the relationship between her and me, I think she would have spoken up and said that there were some things going on. I doubt that she would have said anything to her teachers at school or whatever, but with someone she had a relationship with, I think she would have said something if she had been asked.

D. Did you ever want to confess – and if you did, what stopped you?

M. Yes, I did, but fear wouldn't let me. I was trapped. There was nothing I could do about it without blowing my family apart – which has happened.

D. According to my research, one of the characteristics of child molesters is that they don't pay attention to normal societal boundaries. Were you aware that you were breaking societal barriers, or did you just not care, or what?

M. I don't think I was aware that I was breaking societal barriers.

D. So you weren't aware that it was improper to go into a child's bedroom?

M. No. Not really. I was much more comfortable with children than with adults. I think it's because with adults you can't be completely open and honest; but with kids you can, and I enjoyed that. So it was a lack of maturity. That and the fact that my guilt prevented me from being able to relax with adults.

D. Did you find that you could express yourself more with kids?

M. No, I would draw them out. I wouldn't talk about my deep feelings with them. I would just talk about them.

D. *What would have stopped you from touching a child in the first place?*

M. If they had said no. Saying no and crying. In both cases, with both of the girls, that was it. That was what stopped it with both of them. Now – will that stop every child molester? No. I don't think so. It's just that I have a soft heart and when reality sunk in that I was hurting these children, then I stopped.

D. *Did you ever hear on TV or on the radio about the consequences of molesting a child?*

M. All the time.

D. *How did that affect you?*

M. I'd just quiver and shake inside and be glad that I hadn't gotten caught.

D. *But you proceeded anyway. Why?*

M. Just lack of self-will. I'd just always make myself think, well, she appears to like it, so.... I mean it was delusional, but that's what I did.

D. *Did you want to be caught?*

M. I wanted to stop. I didn't want to get caught. I just couldn't figure out how to stop.

D. *Did you ever try to seek help in any way?*

M. Yes. I would constantly pray that God would get me out of it. I knew it was wrong and felt very guilty after the fact but just wasn't strong enough to stop it.

D. So if you prayed that God would help you to stop, why do you think He didn't?

M. I think it was just a hollow prayer. It just wasn't sincere. My desire for what I was doing was stronger than my desire to stop.

D. How did you hide your sexual preferences all those years?

M. Just by being very manipulative.

D. Did you feel guilt?

M. Yes.

D. How did you handle that?

M. Just tried to put on a brave face – be someone I wasn't. Basically a mask. I couldn't ever really have an in-depth conversation with anybody for fear something would slip. There was no honesty in anything. It was very depressing. I just buried myself in work projects, and so I was never really around anybody for long. I just kept working and working so I didn't have to think about it. That was my self-preservation mechanism.

D. Do you think people have to be cautious when they see a strong bond between a man and a child?

M. I think people have to be perceptive – not cautious – perceptive. For instance, I have a bad feeling about a fellow who is dating my neighbor now. This is a woman who has two young daughters and this boyfriend. One day when he was leaving, he took one of the girls with him – not both girls – one girl. To me, that was an instant red flag. I wondered why he separated those girls. So I think that if you want to protect a child, you have to watch how things are orchestrated and understand manipulation.

D. *When you questioned the situation, should you have confronted the people, or should you have just let the car drive away as you did and hope for the best?*

M. I am going to speak to my counselor about it, but I am in a very delicate position in my neighborhood. There are people, I would say the majority of people, who are rational and understand the nature of forgiveness and are giving me a second chance. There are a few, however, who are really upset about me being there. They haven't vocalized their concerns to me, but I sense the vibe. Most of them are giving me a chance. It's a hard situation.

D. *So you feel that in your position you really can't address it. But for someone else who was concerned, do you think the fellow should have been challenged?*

M. Well it was with the full approval of the mom. She went out to his car and opened the door for the little girl to get in and then let them go off on their own. I guess that in my situation right now, I'm just paranoid. I could be over-reacting to this situation with the mother and her boyfriend because friends of the pair who seem to be people of good judgment don't appear to have a problem with it. They seem to think it's okay. Anyway, a parent just has to be wise.

D. *A lot of people think child-molestation is evil, in the sense of involving demonic activity. Did you ever feel that there was any kind of demonic presence influencing you or harassing you or whatever?*

M.. No. I think Satan gets blamed for a lot of things he doesn't do. This was just selfish human nature.

D. *What was it like being accused of child molestation?*

M. Gut wrenching. My heart stopped. My mind was spinning thinking, well, this won't be that hard to get out of, because there's no hard evidence. That was my initial instinct, but before I admitted that I was guilty, I started realizing that whether I was proven guilty or not, people were going to think I was because I had been accused. The reality was slow to seep in, but when it did, I started to realize that I had to do the right thing.

D. Describe your experience with the law. What was it like when the police came to the door?

M. Initially I had no idea what was going on, but my heart went into my stomach. They were very professional. I don't think they believed the accusations at all at first, mainly because they were so nice to me. I would have thought that if they had, I would have been incarcerated, at least overnight. But after taking me to the station for an interview, they took me home. They were very good to me. There were two uniformed officers and one plainclothesman. They were very professional. I lied through my teeth in the first interview. I was very scared. I think I did a pretty good job of hiding it, but I was really scared.

When I went back the second time (five days later) to confess, it was a huge relief. I felt much, much better about the situation. I finally felt I had done the right thing after a long, long time.

D. What led you to turn yourself in and confess?

M. I realized that this was not going to play out well. That it was going to divide the family and betray them more than I already had. By me denying everything, it was more abuse on Linda. To drag her through a trial was unthinkable. I most likely could have won, if I had played it cool and calculated and denied, denied, denied. If I had continued to lawyer up and done everything they told me to do, I could probably have beat it – but there would have been a big mess in the family and I just really.... I knew I was going away for a long time and I wasn't coming back. I was just going to plead guilty to everything. I didn't care if I went away for life. I knew the best thing for me to do was admit it. Take the lumps.

D. In case someone who is fantasizing about molesting a child reads this interview, I'd like them to understand the price they'll pay. Could you tell exactly what happened from the time you turned yourself in to the police?

M. After making my statement, I was put into a solitary holding cell at the O.P.P. station. I was so relieved finally to have the truth out. There was a nice old lady working there, and so I started to talk to her and told her how good I felt to have done the right thing. She stood there and asked me what the charges were, and I told her. She just went white and became very belligerent and got right on the phone. The constable who I had been talking with came up to my cell and said, "I'm only going to tell you this once. When you go over to the jail, keep your mouth *shut*. People do not want to know about this charge, and so for your own self-preservation, ..." And it was very good advice.

But then, when they took me over to the jail, the guards over there already knew. And so all of this stuff started to happen.

D. That lady told them?

M. I don't know. The guards who carry you over have a record of what you're charged with so that they can process you in. So it started with the strip-search with the guards berating me and marching me naked, carrying my jail clothes, in front of everybody in the holding cells with them all yelling at me about how they were going to get me.... I really... I really don't want to go there.

D. Remember, the reason why I'm asking you about the details of this is in hopes that it will be a deterrent to anyone else who is thinking about molesting a child, and so that victims will feel that they have had some justice.

M. Yeah. It's hell on earth. You can't believe how alone you are. I basically went nuts for a little while. They psychologically broke me. I was delusional for a couple of days at least.

D. What did they do to break you?

M. No sleep. They put me in a padded blanket-garment sort of dress thing with straps made from safety belt fabric over my shoulders. I was strapped into it. I had no clothes. They had taken everything I had. They control the temperature in the cells, and so they turned my heat right down so that it was a very cold cell. All I had was a tiny little blanket about two feet by four feet, made of the same fabric as this dress thing. It was basically what they call their "suicide watch." There was one guard watching me. I don't know his name, but I'll never forget his face. He was a guy who was big in the union and very belligerent. It was that guy who made the decision that I was going to go into the cold cell. I was taken to a nurse, and out of the corner of my eye, I caught him giving her a big wink that this was going to happen.

So they kept me there for three days. Basically, they would stay outside my door and taunt me and tell me how terrible I was. They'd carry on conversations outside my door about all the horrible things they'd heard I did. If I did go to sleep at all, they'd bang on my door to make me wake up. So I'd had no sleep at all and was very, very cold for three days.

Then at five in the morning, they took me down to a holding cell to wait until 8:30 to be loaded into a paddy wagon to go to the courthouse. So I was just left there to wait in this absolutely filthy cell. I think they must smear these places with excrement on purpose so that they are as miserable as they can possibly be. The walls are just covered with feces.

D. You mean in the cells below the courthouse?

M. No – in the Super Jail, but the courtroom cells are the same. There are some cells that are okay, and then there are others that are just terrible. When I was first going through all that, I was always put in the worst ones for obvious reasons. It's like a game to some of these people. The worst guards were the women, by far, but in general, there a lot of very, very good people there.

D. What was the "perp walk?"

M. After they strip search you, they're supposed to give you an orange jumpsuit with underwear and slippers and you should be able to put those on, because there are five or six low-walled cement cubicles so that when you return from court, you're supposed to strip out of your street clothes back into the prison wear in those cubicles. But instead of that, when a prisoner like me is taken from the holding cell to the regular cells, they make them stay naked, just carrying their prison clothes and walk past all these holding cells, some of which can hold as many as 30 men. Some hold ten or twenty and then there are some cells with just one man. They let these guys know what the charges are and so as I walked down the hall, all these guys were yelling profanities and threats about how they were going to get me. It was... So that was the perp walk.

D. So that happened when you first got there?

M. I turned myself in on Saturday morning and spent Saturday night in a holding cell in the O.P.P. Station. Sunday morning, I did video court from there. Then I was transported to the Super Jail Sunday afternoon, and that's where the perp walk and everything else started.

That's when I was taken up to the psyche ward and put in the cold cell for three days, supposedly on suicide watch. But every time I was taken back and forth to court, it was like a perp walk because the other prisoners were made aware of what the charges were.

D. Did you ever find yourself in grave danger?

M. Yes. Many times. There were times when I could have been killed – people who wanted to kill me. But God was there and protected me the whole time.

D. You've talked about being active in a church. How could you call yourself a Christian?

M. I had committed my life to God and believed everything in the Bible. I just wasn't following what it said. I put my own desires ahead of everything and didn't work at applying Scripture to my life. I was just a guy sitting in a pew saying all the right things but doing whatever I felt like doing.

D. Did you feel as though God had left you in prison?

M. No, although I certainly deserved to have Him leave me. There were so many occurrences when really bad things could have happened. I could have died. Just on my pod, there were several guys who would have killed me as quick as they would have looked at me if they could have gotten their hands on me. I feel that God gave me wisdom in what to say, what to do and how to react. Whenever I would ask Him what I was to do in a particular situation, I would just feel a flood of peace, and I knew He was with me. I'd do whatever it was I felt He told me to do and I was protected.

D. After all of that, do you still have an attraction to children?

M. No. Quite frankly, I've gone overboard the other way. I'm frightened of children now. If I'm in a grocery store and there are
24

a couple of kids in an aisle without their mother, I'll turn my cart around and go the opposite direction. It's just common good sense. It's not that I'm afraid of re-offending because that's not going to happen. My fear is that I'll be perceived as doing something inappropriate. I'm extremely careful not to put myself in a position where anyone could get the wrong idea.

D. How do you feel about yourself now?

M. I'm just a work in progress. I have difficulty with some things. For instance, in my work, I can't get overly friendly with anybody or invite them to church because if they come, I'll lose my job. Someone there will ask if they know about my background – and that will be it. I'll be history. Any effect I have on people just has to be through the way I live my life, through being a person who is not profane, who is honest and helpful – but I can't invite them to come to my church. That understanding came through the first job I got at a trucking company after I was released. I was the best night watchman they had ever had – until one guy found out that I had been in prison and that was it. So it makes that part of it difficult.

D. How do you feel about yourself now in relation to other people?

M. I feel as though I'll always be in a fishbowl. Everybody is reading behind the lines, wondering what I'm doing. I know my pastor and his church board are pleased that I'm doing everything to earn their respect and keep people comfortable and stick to the reintegration plan without being reminded. For instance, I'd never go to the washroom in the church. If I had to go, I'd leave the building and go home and go there. It's just staying away from any perception of acting questionably.

It's difficult because I can't just go out anywhere and socialize and tell anybody about my past and expect anyone to be supportive because it's just not going to happen. So I'm isolated. I can't just go out and be a normal person. I'm just coming to grips with that now and realizing that that's always the way life is going to be for me. It's my fault – nobody else's.

I do feel very good about my relationship with my parole officer and my psychologist. They are very positive about the support group I have. The fact that my sister and my aunt have been so incredibly supportive says a lot to them and has meant so much in my ability to rebuild my life.

Most of the guys like me don't have the support group I have. They've lost everybody, and they just give up. They re-offend so that they can go back in to get off the streets. They're without any means, and life is just too terrible on the outside.

D. Are you still a manipulator?

M. I don't think so. I hope not. I try to be frank and honest about everything, and I think that is the key. If someone asks me a direct question, I'm not going to lie about it. For instance, if someone were to ask me at my work if I had been in prison for child molestation, I wouldn't lie about it. I'd say yes, and then I might as well go out and get in my car because I'd lose my job. So from that standpoint, I'm not that same person anymore.

I think that's why a few of my old friends and my sister and aunt have stuck by me because there's been a trust factor built up which I greatly cherish. Without it, I'd be lost. I'd be out of my mind, I guess. That's all I can do.

Now, I recognize my lot in life. If I didn't have the backing of my support group, I know I'd be in big trouble. I think I'd just collapse. But I do think that God has brought this support group together. It just seems supernatural to me. I was never that close to my aunt or my sister until this happened.

D. What role does remorse play in your life? How do you deal with the shame?

M. I don't call it remorse. That may sound strange. I call it reality. There are realities that I have to live with for the rest of my life. There is an awareness of how deeply this has adversely affected the people in my life. Their woes right now are caused primarily by me, and I'm aware of that.

Remorse and shame? This has taught me to see the girls as real people with emotions, thoughts, and needs. I betrayed their trust, and I feel very badly because I took advantage of their vulnerability.

D. What will you do if the temptation returns?

M. I'm going at life in such a way as to not allow the temptation to return. I've purposed myself to walk away from any possibly compromising situations.

I read a lot and keep myself busy with work and church. When impure thoughts come into my mind, I replace them with positive, healthy thoughts or good memories. The key is not ignoring bad thoughts – it's replacing them. I know that I can talk to my pastor about anything, anytime. We have both concluded that man, left to his desires, is very dark. We are all tempted but left to run rampant, the imagination can be a disastrous thing.

D. So you'd say to someone else in your position that it's all about trying to transform your mind – trying to get rid of the damage done by your porn addiction?

M. Knowing exactly what the pitfalls are and how to avoid them is critical. Replacing dark thoughts. That's why this verse is so important to me. *"Whatever is true, whatever is noble, whatever is right, whatever is pure, whatever is lovely, whatever is admirable – if anything is excellent or praiseworthy – think about such things."*[2] If a temptation comes into my mind, I immediately capture that thought and replace it with something else – often a memory, like laying on my back, looking up at the stars with one of my grandchildren. That is such a wonderful, solid memory. Or driving down to the lake with my old dog, Jack. The point is that you can't *not* think about something, or it becomes the elephant in the room. It becomes bigger and more important. You have to replace it with something better.

D. If you could say anything to your victims, what would it be?

M. That I'm very sorry. I know that sounds like a very trite thing to say. I wish there had been an opportunity for them to confront me – for everyone who this touched to confront me and be able to express how I hurt them. I know that the victim impact statements are meant to do that, but the girls weren't there when I read them. I would like them to know how sorry I truly am. I don't deserve reconciliation, but in the long haul, it is the only thing that will bring peace to them.

D. Is doing this interview an effort on your part to make some restitution?

M. The best thing I can do for my victims is never to offend again. As the perpetrator, nothing I say means a hill of beans. It's only what I do with the rest of my life that could make some small possible bit of difference to them. I'm aware of that. It may never make any difference, and that thought makes me very sad, but it's a reality.

D. Is there anything I haven't asked?

---

2. Phillippians, Ch. 4, The Bible

M. There are no excuses for anyone to molest a child. No reasons. Every individual is responsible for his or her own choices. Mine were detestably self-gratifying. The road to healing starts with taking responsibility for your actions. All of the repercussions I face were brought on by my own hand. They are no one else's fault.

I turned off the recorder and breathed.

Why Do They Do It??

Why, for goodness sake, would a fully grown married man want to manipulate a child into sexual interaction? It makes no sense. Even if we try to figure it out with a gazillion studies, it doesn't erase the gut-wrenching consequences of the actions of a predator. However, perhaps by trying to understand, some child will be protected.

While healthy humans are born with the propensity to engage in sexual activity, they're not born to be pedophiles or child molesters. Those desires are developed as a result of early experiences or interruptions in normal development.

Everyone needs to be touched and loved. As individuals mature, sexual satisfaction is added to the list of needs. During puberty, boys suddenly become preoccupied with sex. Their sex hormones increase fivefold within a two year period. Whatever sexual messages are delivered to them during that period are naturally going to have great significance. If they have positive interactions with females during that time, they are more likely to develop as heterosexuals. On the other hand, if they are socially awkward and experience sexual arousal with the same sex or with someone considerably younger, it will be remembered as pleasurable, and they may begin to seek out that source of arousal again and again, rather than changing the brain cues and seeking heterosexual satisfaction.

29

Of course, the motivations are different for each person, and they change over time. They are as varied as individual childhoods and early experiences. A rapist or a sadist, for example, is going to differ in motivations from a man who touches the genitals of a single child.

Sometimes, the motivation has nothing to do with sex. For a sadistic rapist, it may be all about hostility and cruelty. For a diddling molester, it may be all about control or power imbalance, perhaps as a reinforcement of his "ownership" of the child; or it could be an authority figure power trip he gets from children.

Jocelyn, the sad-eyed, once-pretty mother of three sons, sat with me one rainy afternoon and recounted her heart-breaking experience. With too many lines etched on her face, she told me about her precious middle son who had been molested by a close family friend.

My son's molester claimed that his father molested him, so it felt natural. He said he was just "teaching (my son) about sex." When I heard those words, I was enraged - *enraged!* How *dare* he rob my son of the carefree innocence of childhood! How *dare* he rob me of my parental privilege and responsibility before my son was old enough to know about such things! How *dare* he masquerade helpfulness for selfishness! How *dare* he impose himself on my son as the first experience with sex! How *dare* he dupe me into believing that his home was the safest place in the world for my little boy to be? How *dare* he express his darkest, most vile imaginings on my sweet child? How *dare* he carry on a relationship with my family for years, hiding this terrible secret? How *dare* he subject my son to the lifelong challenges of a molested child? How *dare* he pretend to be such an upstanding, charming member of society?

She paused and then continued.

I never thought I would be able to smile again. My child's molester seemed to think it was just fine to use whoever was accessible to involve in his sex life. And yet he *knew* it was wrong because he kept it hidden. He seemed to have no concept of respect for boundaries.

Dr. Jeckyll – Mr. Hyde

A pedophile can be an unshaven stranger who hangs around playgrounds, obviously scoping out his prey; or perhaps he is the executive on the 34th floor, or a neighbor like Matt, or a husband with whom one has lived for fifty years.

Some data suggests that up to one-third of child molesters are female.[3] Accurate statistics are impossible to compile because abuse by women is often not reported and often not considered abuse. While contradictory studies show that number to be much smaller, we do know that the majority are men.

Despite child advocate John Walsh's advice to parents never to hire a male baby-sitter, it's important not to marginalize men. Some go so far as to say that people who refuse to hire male nannies (mannies) are practicing male profiling, not unlike police who pull drivers over for DWH (Driving While Hispanic or Hungarian). While it's important to foster warm relationships between healthy men and children, a refusal to hire a male baby sitter is not about equal rights or profiling; it's just about minimizing risk. Having said that, for the sake of simplicity, most references are to "he" in this booklet.

---

3. Van Dam, Carla (2001). *Identifying Child Molesters, Preventing Child Sexual Abuse by Recognizing the Patterns of the Offenders,* New York: The Halworth Maltreatment and Trauma Press, p.56.

A child molester can be a doctor, a garbage-collector, a teacher, a musician, a son, a brother, a teenager, a senior, a billionaire, a pauper, a homosexual, a heterosexual, a Christian, a Buddhist or an agnostic. He can be fighting trim or flabby; American, French, Russian or Oriental. He can be the recognized ex-convict down the street who has served his time – or he can be the man next door whose worst known offense was a speeding ticket when he was 16. He can be the gentle grandpa or the personable baby-sitter.

Parents used to warn their little ones not to talk to strangers. However, today's research relegates stranger danger to a smaller role. Tragically, the highest incidence of child sexual abuse is within the family. In L. Halliday's research[4] on over 1,000 subjects, only 13 percent of the abuse was committed by strangers. Fifty-seven percent was committed by family members and 28 percent involved friends. Twenty-one percent involved natural fathers, 12 percent stepfathers, 10 percent uncles, 10 percent brothers, five percent grandfathers, 19 percent family friends and three percent baby-sitters. Children in step-families are at higher risk because, with the addition of more extended family, more people have easy access to them. It's impossible to document exact numbers or demographics because so many incidents go unreported and study results differ.

One thing is clear: the stereotype of the "dirty old man" is misleading. The majority of offenders are under the age of 35.[5]

In a 1986 interview in *The New York Times*, Ted Bundy, one of America's worst killers – a handsome, articulate law student working in the Republican party, said, "What people have to realize is that...

---

4. Halliday, L. (1985). Sexual Abuse: Counseling issues and concerns. Campbell River, B.C., Ptarmigan Press.
5. Abel, G., Becker, J., Mittleman, M., Rouleau, J., and Murphy, W. (1987). Journal of Interpersonal Violence, 2(1), March, p.3-25.

in all significant respects, I am essentially like everybody else." His lawyer, James Coleman said, "He's your next-door neighbor. People don't want to believe their next-door neighbor can behave like this."

Unless convicted, pedophiles don't come with labels that warn people. Even if convicted, the labels mean little because it's impossible to know whether the bearers will ever offend again. It is possible that the least dangerous man is the one who has been caught, served his time and dealt with his dark heart in a genuine way. It is possible that the most dangerous person is the unsuspected man who sits beside one in a sports arena.

Child molester or pedophile?

It can be helpful to know that child molesters are not necessarily pedophiles and pedophiles are not necessarily child molesters. Pedophilia is a psychological disorder defined by a distinct sexual preference for pre-pubescent children. The Diagnostic and Statistical Manual of Mental Disorders, published by the American Psychological Association, gives the following definition of pedophilia:

> "Recurrent, intense, sexual urges and sexually arousing fantasies of at least six months duration involving sexual activity with a pre-pubescent child."[6]

Thus, an individual can be a pedophile without actually engaging in a sexual act. Simply having fantasies about sexual activity with a child over a period of at least six months will qualify. Many pedophiles never engage in any actual criminal activity. They just stay at home and think about it. They often have large collections of

---

6. Diagnostic and Statistical Manual of Mental Disorders (DSM 111-R), The American Psychological Association, 1987.

child pornography or child erotica. Staying close to children is high on their list of priorities. The most common type of pedophile is the immature individual who has never been very successful maintaining peer relationships. Those who lack social contact often spiral down deeper and deeper into a fantasy world.

Pedophiles who physically engage in child molestation become "child molesters." They often use their collections of erotica and pornography to show to their victims as part of the grooming process of seduction. They think that when their victims see the photographs, their inhibitions will be lowered and they'll be more inclined to accept sexual activity as something people normally do. Some use photographs and videos they have made of their victims to blackmail them into further sexual activity.

Child molesters, on the other hand, by definition engage in sexual acts with children, but most of them will go after older victims as well. Ninety-five percent of them are male. Only ten percent are strangers to their victims. Fifty to 60 percent are family members. According to a Public Health Agency of Canada fact sheet, 25 percent of molesters are teenagers. The rule of thumb used by professionals is that child sexual abuse occurs when a person touches a child for sexual gratification and is four years older than the child. (Curious playmates of the same age are protected by the age issue.)

Because family members are often hidden from the criminal justice system, it's difficult for researchers to get a handle on the true extent of the problem. They have been more successful in characterizing family friends and trusted adults outside of the family. These people usually don't use violence on their victims. Like Matt, they "groom" them, or set them up for the molestation by gradually establishing bonds with the child. By the time the first touch happens, the child has been so conditioned that he or she doesn't recognize the danger.

Molesters victimize children for other motives as well as sexual gratification. Sometimes it's just part of the mistreatment they direct toward people in general. Usually, they have low self-esteem and view children as less powerful objects on which to vent their anger or sexual frustrations. The main criteria for choosing a victim is availability. It could be anyone, anywhere, who happens to be in the wrong place at the wrong time. Predators can be strangers who forcefully attack children they don't know, or individuals or family members, known to the child, who use the situation to their own advantage with no concern for the victim.

Those child molesters who prefer sex with children can have an astounding number of victims over a lifetime, if not caught. They choose particular victims and groom them for abuse through developing a relationship of trust, buying them gifts and honing in on their emotional weaknesses. According to U.S. Department of Justice statistics, in more than 90 percent of cases of child rape, the offender was well-known to the children or their parents. These are pedophiles who have carried their fantasies into reality. Some are brutal and physically cruel, while others are more gentle in their approaches. They manipulate relationships to the point of expressing their perversions.

The Newest Twist to the Oldest Perversion

In 1874, the police in London, England, arrested a photographer with 130,000 pornographic images of children.[7] In those days, the images were on glass plates. Child pornography is nothing new. Stories of incest filter way back in biblical times to the story of Lot and his daughters.

---

7. Sher, Julian, *One Child at a Time*, Random House Canada, p.36.

What is new is that pedophiles are becoming increasingly empowered through the use of the Internet. They used to be a solitary lot, isolated by the shame of their perversions and repressed by the revulsion of normal society.

But now they can go online and, with a click of the mouse, find like-minded people with whom to share not only photographs but actual live occurrences of child rape and molestation. While Booklet #5 in this series, *The Porn Factor*, addresses this more fully, the point here is that pedophiles are no longer the isolated loners they once were. Thanks to the Internet, they are part of a slimy club of peers they can access at any moment, day or night, and feed their perversions. Because of the group solidarity, they feel more legitimized and thus are becoming bolder and bolder. Because of the group dynamic, they are interacting more like a repressed minority than an intolerable plague on society.

Victims as Child Molesters

A study by Briggs and Hawkins[8] found that sex abusers who were abused themselves as children often regarded their own abuse as "normal," sometimes even enjoyable in a confused way.

In contrast, the non-offenders they studied who had been abused as children, were more likely to report their own abuse as negative. Thus the study speculated that men who normalized their personal experiences of sexual abuse could be more likely to become abusers themselves, and then fail to understand the harm they caused.

While the study revealed that more than 93 percent of convicted

---

8. Briggs, F., & Hawkins, R.M.F. (1996). A comparison of the childhood experiences of convicted male child molesters and men who were sexually abused in childhood and claimed to be non offenders. Child Abuse and Neglect, 20, 221-33.

child molesters suffered abuse as children[9], being a victim of sexual abuse does not naturally lead to being an offender as an adult. There are far too many victims for that to be the case. It is estimated that up to 48 million women and up to 22 million men in the United States have suffered molestation before the age of 18. Also, the fact that more than twice as many women as men are victimized, while most of the molesters are men, does not gel with the theory of the victim necessarily becoming a victimizer.

Sadly, many molesters or potential molesters never disclose the abuse they themselves have received, thus short-circuiting any possibility of treatment before acting out their fantasies.

Part of the purpose of marriage is to help each other heal from the wounds of childhood. In my own case, my ex-husband was so trapped in the secrecy of his pornography and activities that opportunities to interact in healthy, healing ways weren't there.

Thoughts of "if only I had..." are sad refrains sung by countless unsuspecting families of convicted molesters who wish they had been given the opportunity to help the offender to heal, prior to his descent into criminality. In many cases, if they had had the chance to intervene, precious children would not have had to suffer...

Whatever the reasons for the criminal behavior, we can only try to get a handle on the "why," so that if we catch a glimpse of someone developing this kind of mindset, we can try to divert his or her course for the protection of some unknown child sometime, somewhere.

Recognize the Warning Signs

---

9. Briggs, F., & Hawkins, R.M.F. (1996). A comparison of the childhood experiences of convicted male child molesters and men who were sexually abused in childhood and claimed to be non offenders. Child Abuse and Neglect, 20, 221-33.

While it is often a total shock to those who know him when a pedophile or a child molester is revealed, there are sometimes signs that no one wants to recognize until they are no longer possible to ignore.

For instance, Janice (name changed), the wife of a convicted molester, told me that it always bothered her that whenever they went to visit friends, her husband would seem to want to spend more time with the children than with the adults. In her words:

> It was embarrassing because I felt he was sending a message to our hosts that they weren't interesting enough for him. He thought nothing of leaving a room of adults to spend time with children, sometimes in their rooms. To me, it was highly inappropriate to go anywhere in someone else's house without an adult leading the way – but the trespassing of accepted social boundaries didn't seem to faze him. If I were to complain on the way home, he would deny having spent an inappropriately greater amount of time with the children than with the adults, making me feel like a prissy complainer. Because there was no evidence of him actually doing anything to a child, my discomfort regarding his behavior was limitied to confusion and frustration. Eventually, it became easier to stay home than to socialize and have to risk offending our friends – or have them wonder about my husband...to say nothing of going home in an argument.

Mallory, another wife of a convicted molester said,

> It bothered me that whenever young girls would visit my grandchildren, Joseph would seem more interested in them than I felt was normal. I chalked it up to him being

emotionally immature, the result of some unknown influence
that had kept him trapped in adolescence. Whenever young
female friends needed transportation or help of any kind, he
was right there, offering to help before having to be asked.
With my busy life, I appreciated his helpfulness enormously.
The children always seemed to love his attentions, and it made
me feel like a spoil-sport if I were to complain. I remembered
all of my uncles who had given me such a lovely sense of
importance in this world, and tried to reassure myself that
Joseph was doing the same for these children.

Many mothers and grandmothers might think such a willing spirit
was too good to be true. For these women, it was.

Mallory went on to say,

One of the young girls who was a frequent visitor in our
home came from a dysfunctional family. Lacking the stability
and attention she needed, she responded wholeheartedly to
Joseph's attentions and was forever wanting to sit on his knee,
comb his hair and be with him wherever he went. If I were
to try to deter her or voice any discomfort about it, Joseph
would remind me that she needed a sense of security and the
knowledge that she was special to people.

Looking back, it's more than obvious to me that I was naïve.
But at the time, I didn't dream Joseph would actually *do*
anything inappropriate. My fear was that someone might
incorrectly suspect his motives because his behavior wasn't
normal; it was never that he would ever actually molest a
child! In my heart of hearts, I believed him to be foolishly
opening himself up for suspicion – *never dreaming* that
any suspicion would be grounded. He angered me with his

stupidity. I felt that I had to protect him from people who might not understand how harmless, helpful and loving he was. I thought he was just a big, gentle teddy bear.

In retrospect, sadly, painfully, the warning signs were clear.

Dr. Charles Whitfield found that the most effective cover a child molester has is the *desire* of people not to know. When offenders deny their guilt, people want so much to believe that it didn't happen that it resonates with their personal beliefs about the incident.

Manipulative molesters play on the doubts of normal people that someone who appears respectable would ever do such a horrible thing. Because people don't want to believe it, if someone they care about is charged with a sexual crime, they try desperately to find some other logical explanation for the child's disclosure. Because the majority of people are more trusting than suspicious, particularly if the people in question are attractive and polite, they unknowingly enable child molesters to harm children.

In the course of researching her book, *Identifying Child Molesters*,[10] Dr. Carla van Dam interviewed over 300 molesters who exhibited similar types of behaviors in social situations. While there is no precise profile to identify predators, these similar behaviors provide us with a general pattern. If an individual exhibits enough of these behaviors to arouse concern, he or she needs to be considered too risky to be allowed to be unsupervised around our children.

No predator will exhibit all of the signs common to molesters, simply because of human individuality. However, he or she will usually exhibit a combination of the signs in the following list:

---

10. Van Dam, Carla (2001). *Identifying Child Molesters, Preventing Child Sexual Abuse by Recognizing the Patterns of the Offenders*, New York: The Halworth Maltreatment and Trauma Press.

- There will be a general feeling of discomfort in the presence of the person in question.

- An emotionally dysfunctional adult may pay particular attention to a needy child.

- He may show a preference for association with children.

- The person in question maintains few friendships in his own age bracket.

- He has structured access to children. In order to groom a child and his or her parents for the abuse, a child molester has to have a legitimate connection to the child that will allow for the process of time the "grooming" takes. Teaching, bus driving, sports coaching, camp counseling and volunteering to help with children's activities, all offer opportunities to be alone with children with no parental supervision.

- He encourages a child to develop feelings, entrapping the young victim in a situation where the child feels that the abuse is legitimized by his or her feelings for the abuser. This is a psychological process known as the "Stockholm Syndrome" where victims develop feelings of attachment to their captors. (As the victims mature, the affection for the abuser usually dwindles, and the painful truth emerges.)

- The person in question may have frequent changes of residence or jobs without much discussion about the reasons for the changes.

- While pedophiles most often have failed marriages because of their sexual preference, they often stay in the marriage to mask their true intentions. The mate becomes a "front" for a respectable life. While they may indicate to the wife that they

41

simply have no interest in sex, the reality may be quite the opposite.

- There may be a continuation of inappropriate association with children despite concerns expressed by others.

- They may appear disconnected from normal peers.

- They may refer to children in particularly exalted terms, such as "beautiful," "adorable," or other labels that are said in a way that seems excessive.

- They may seem to have disrespect for social boundaries.

- They may exhibit behavior that seems too good to be true, perhaps being overly helpful.

- They may have a desire for hobbies that seem more appropriate for a child than for an adult, like building miniature trains, collecting toys or whatever.

- They may have either a particularly charming personality or obvious 'loner' qualities, sometimes a combination of both. The charmers are socially appealing but often lack substance in their relationships. There's no sense of genuine bonding at a heart level.

- Lack of development of the capacity for intimacy, resulting in emotional loneliness.

- There may be interaction with young teens at a peer level, engaging in conversations about sex, crushes or whatever would not normally be of interest for an adult to discuss with a teen.

- Playing with children at a peer level; tickling, play fighting, etc., to gain confidence and rapport and introduce the child to touching.

As the child becomes desensitized to touch in appropriate places, the touch progresses to breasts and genitals.

• Response to concerns about denial and aggression, making the concerned individual feel like a fool

• Maintenance of an image of social acceptability, often taking leadership in children's groups through which to gain the trust of parents and children alike.

Any of these warning signs need to be viewed within the context of an individual's life. For instance, if someone enjoys playing with children *in the company of other adults*, that's normal. If someone is a particularly helpful person but *doesn't seek out the company of children*, that's a wonderful thing. However, if combinations of the above qualities are evident, there's cause for concern and children need to be carefully watched around these people.

The alarming revelations of hundreds of men in the 1990's and 2000's of childhood sexual molestation by Catholic priests are sad testimonies to the compulsions of some predators who live their whole lives victimizing children until the day they are caught. Some have a history of using hundreds of children over their lifetimes. Such revelations have been shattering, but in Booklet #4 – *Predators in Pews and Pulpits,* it will become evident that one denomination is no purer than any other regarding to abuse.

The Manipulative Molester

One characteristic shared by all child molesters is that they are finely tuned manipulators, and they recognize their adeptness at manipulating people to achieve their ends.

During my ex-husband's confession, he said, "I am the world's greatest manipulator." While that claim could have been debatable, the statement was evidence of the cancerous quality of his approach to relationships. Finally, my inability to connect with him, despite years of trying, made sense. Nothing had been real. Whenever I tried to connect with him on a deep heart level, he would shrug his shoulders and say, "I'm not a very deep guy. What you see is all there is."

Manipulative men hide in plain sight. They hide their true selves from everyone.

In her book, *The Manipulative Man*, Dorothy McCoy referred to the ICD-10 (the mental health manual used in Europe) in listing the following characteristics[11] to watch for in classifying someone as a manipulator:

- Callous unconcern for the feelings of others
- Gross and persistent attitude of irresponsibility and disregard for social norms, rules, and obligations
- Incapacity to maintain enduring relationships, though having no difficulty in establishing them
- Very low tolerance to frustration and a low threshold for discharge of aggression, including violence
- Incapacity to experience guilt or to profit from experience, particularly punishment
- Marked proneness to blame others, or to offer plausible rationalizations, for the behavior that has brought the patient into conflict with society.

While these are guidelines for identification, not every manipulator will exhibit all of the characteristics, and those who do will do so in greater and lesser degrees.

---

11. McCoy, D. (2006). *The Manipulative Man*, Adams Media, Avon, Mass. p.9.

Although most manipulators are aware of rules and taboos, they have no respect for them. The fact that they are so crafty in hiding their deeds demonstrates that they know very well that what they are doing is wrong.

The "Moment"

Whether or not a perpetrator is discovered and incarcerated, there is a "moment" when he or she has to admit that the consequences of his or her choices are so bad that life is out of control.

For a public figure, this may be the news-making moment when flashbulbs are popping as the police escort him from his house to a waiting cruiser.

For a father, it may be the moment his son finds his stash of porn.

For a priest, minister or rabbi, it could be the first moment alone as he lies on his hard cell mattress.

Who is the Predator?

Who is the predator? Only she or he knows – until the silence is broken.

We are called the "guardians" of our children because we must always stand on guard for them, daring to face the reality that those we know and love may not be beyond falling prey to the darkest inclinations of their hearts.

Do we have to live in fear and paranoia? No. We can live in a spirit of love for our fellow man; the knowledge that we, as parents, grandparents, and community are empowered through diligence to protect our children. With soundness of mind, we can overcome the fallout from darkness.

For further reading...

Abel, G., Becker, J., Mittleman, M., Rouleau, J., and Murphy, W. (1987). Journal of Interpersonal Violence, 2(1), March

Beauregard, M and O'Leary, D. (2007). The Spiritual Brain, A Neuroscientist's Case for the Existence of the Soul, HarperOne, San Francisco, CA

The Holy Bible, The New International Version, Zondervan Bible Publishers, Grand Rapids, Michigan.

Birchall, E. (1989). The Frequency of Child Abuse – What do We Really Know?, in Colton, Matthew and Vanstone, Maurice (1996). Betrayal of Trust; Sexual Abuse by Men Who Work With Children, , London ON: Free Association Books Ltd.

Bremner, Dr. J. Douglas (2007). The Lasting Effects of Psychological Trauma on Memory and the Hippocampus, Law and Psychiatry,

Briggs, F., & Hawkins, R.M.F. (1996). A comparison of the childhood experiences of convicted male child molesters and men who were sexually abused in childhood and claimed to be non offenders. Child Abuse and Neglect

Browne, A., & Finkelhor, D. (1986). Initial and long-term effects: A review of the research. In D. Finkelhor, A Sourcebook on Child Sexual Abuse, Beverly Hills: Sage

Bushman, B.J., Baumeister, R.F., & Stack, A.D. (1999). Catharsis, aggression and persuasive influence: Self-fulfilling or self-defeating prophecies? Journal of Personality and Social Psychology

Butler, Sandra (1985). Conspiracy of Silence: The Trauma of Incest, San Francisco, Volcano Press.

Carnes, Patrick (1994). Out of the Shadows; Understanding Sexual Addiction, Center City, Minnesota: Hazelden Foundation

Carter, Wm. Lee (2002). A Teen's Guide to Overcoming Sexual Abuse; It Happened to Me, Oakland, Ca., New Harbinger Publications, Inc.

Colton, Matthew and Vanstone, Maurice (1996). Betrayal of Trust; Sexual

Abuse by Men Who Work With Children, , London ON: Free Association Books Ltd.

Diagnostic and Statistical Manual of Mental Disorders (DSM 111-R), The American Psychological Association, 1987

Elliott, M., Browne, K., & Kilcoyne, J. (1995). Child Sexual Abuse Prevention: What Offenders Tell Us, Child Abuse & Neglect

Fink, Paul (2005). Science, Vol. 309, August.

Finkelhor, D. (1984). Child Sexual Abuse: New Theory and Research, New York: Free Press.

Finkelhor, D. and associates (eds) (1986), A Sourcebook on Child Sexual Abuse, Newbury Park, CA.: Sage.

Finkelhor, D., Hotaling, G., Lewis, I. and Smith, C. (1990) Sexual Abuse in a National Survey of Adult Men and Women; Prevalence Characteristics and Risk Factors, Child Abuse and Neglect.

Finkelhor, D. (1994). The International epidemiology of child sexual abuse. Child Abuse & Neglect, 18

Finkelhor, D. and Dziuba-Leatherman, J. (1995). Victimization prevention programs: A national survey of children's exposure and reactions, Child Abuse & Neglect

Finney, Lynne D. (1992). Reach for the Rainbow; Advance Healing for Survivors of Sexual Abuse, New York: The Putnam Publishing Group

Forward, Susan, and Craig Buck (1979). Betrayal of Innocence: Incest and its Devastation, New York: Penguin Books.

Genesee Justice Family (2005). Genesee Justice 2005; Instruments of Law, Order and Peace, Batavia, N.Y., Genesee Justice Family Research & Development

Groth, N., Burgess, A., Birnbaum, H. and Gary, T. (1978). A study of the child molester. Myths and realities. LAE Journal of the American Criminal Justice Association, 41(1), Winter/Spring.

Halliday, L. (1985). Sexual Abuse: Counseling issues and concerns. Campbell River, B.C., Ptarmigan Press

Hergenhahn, B.R. (1992). An introduction to the history of psychology. Belmont, CA:Wadsworth Publishing Company.

Hopper, Dr. J. (2007). Child Abuse: Statistics, Research and Resources Jacob Wetterling Foundation web site's frequently asked questions section

Knopp, Fay Honey (1982). Remedial Intervention in Adolescent Sex Offenses; Nine Program Descriptions, Brooklyn, N.Y.: Faculty Press, Inc.

Leaf , Dr. Caroline (2007). Who Switched Off My Brain?, Switch on Your Brain, Rivonia, South Africa

Lilienfeld, Scott O. and Lambert, Kelly (Oct. 2007). Brain Stains, Scientific American

MacAulay, The Honourable Lawrence - Solicitor General Canada (2001). High-Risk Offenders; A Handbook for Criminal Justice Professionals, Ottawa, The Government of Canada

Marshall, Dr. W.L. and Barrett, Sylvia (1990). Criminal Neglect; Why Sex Offenders Go Free, Toronto: Doubleday Canada Limited

Matthews, Dr. Frederick (1995). Breaking Silence - Creating Hope; Help for Adults Who Molest Children, Ottawa: National Clearinghouse on Family Violence, Health Canada

McCoy, D. (2006). The Manipulative Man, Adams Media, Avon, Mass

Mercy, J. A. (1999). Having New Eyes: Viewing Child Sexual Abuse as a Public Health Problem. Sexual Abuse: A Journal of Research and Treatment

Michel, Lou and Herbeck, Dan, Confessions of a Child Porn Addict, The Buffalo News, Oct. 21, 2007

Minnery, Tom (1986). Pornography; A Human Tragedy, Wheaton, Illinois, Tyndale House Publishers Inc., Dr. J. Dobson

Murr, Doris C. (2004). Dorie's Secret, Kitchener, Ontario, Pandora Press

Peck, M. Scott (1983). People of the Lie, New York, Touchstone - Simon & Schuster Inc.

Posten, Carol and Lison, Karen (1990). Reclaiming our Lives; Hope for

Adult Survivors of Incest, Boston, MA: Little, Brown & Company

Pryor, Douglas W. (1996). Unspeakable Acts; Why men Sexually Abuse Children, New York and London: New York University Press

Public Health Agency of Can. (2007), Nat. Clearinghouse on Family Violence.

Reavill, Gil (2005). Smut; A Sex Industry Insider (and Concerned father) says Enough is Enough, London, England, Penguin Books, Ltd.

Rush, F. (1980). The best kept secret: Sexual abuse of children. New York, McGraw-Hill Book Company

The San Francisco Chronicle (April 3, 2005)

Salter, Anna C. (1988). Treating Child Sex Offenders and Victims; A Practical Guide, Newbury Park, California: SAGE Publications, Inc.

Salter, Anna C. (2003). Predators: Pedophiles, Rapists and Other Sex Offenders , New York: Basic Books

Science Daily, July 30, 2007. News release issued by Stanford University Medical Centre

Seligman, M.E.P. (1994). What You Can Change and What You Can't. New York: Alfred A. Knopf.

Sher, Julian (2007). One Child at a Time, Random House Canada

Singer, P. (1991). Ethics. The New Encyclopedia Britannica, Volume 18, Edition 15

UN Secretary General's Study on Violence Against Children (2006) section II.B

Van Dam, Carla (2001). Identifying Child Molesters, Preventing Child Sexual Abuse by Recognizing the Patterns of the Offenders, New York: The Halworth Maltreatment and Trauma Press

Wholey, Sam (1992). When the Worst That Can Happen Already Has; Conquering Life's Most Difficult Times, New York: Hyperion

Yantzi, Mark (1998). Sexual Offending and Restoration, Waterloo, Ontario and Scottdale, Pa., Herald Press

About Diane Roblin-Lee (Rutledge)

Diane Roblin-Lee, award-winning author, former social-worker and educator, has (out of personal heartbreak) done extensive research in the field of child sexual abuse and the role played by pornography.

Having written over twenty books on a variety of subjects, Diane's passion has always been for the family – not only her own, but also in recognition of its importance as the basic unit of society. With the theme of family running through all of her work, Diane has been politically active, hosted several TV programs (including NiteLite for seven years) and served for many years on the board of the Heart to Heart Marriage and Family Institute.

Her legacy journal, *To My Family...My Life Legacy,* is a priceless resource for those wishing to bless their families with the insights, wisdom and experience gained through their lifetimes.

Remarried in 2021, Diane and her husband, Glen Rutledge, are committed to helping to ensure the protection of children everywhere, through whatever means possible. Glen was the founder of Circle Square TV and Circle Square Ranches for kids across Canada. They are currently building LifeNet Ministries Inc., a suicide prevention initiative for young people.
www.lifenet4hope.com

For further information on

Training Workshops and Speakers
Information and Training Materials, please contact:

Plan to Protect ®
117 Ringwood Dr., Unit #11
Stouffville, ON CAN L4A 8C1
www.plantoprotect.com 1-877-455-3555

Other Books by Diane
can be seen at
www.bydesignmedia.ca
and
amazon.com/author/dianeroblinlee

www.ingramcontent.com/pod-product-compliance
Lightning Source LLC
Chambersburg PA
CBHW060524280326
41933CB00014B/3093